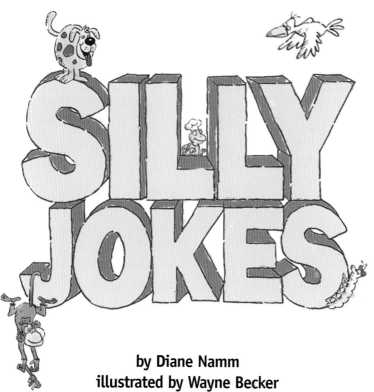

SILLY JOKES

by Diane Namm
illustrated by Wayne Becker

BARNES
& NOBLE
BOOKS

NEW YORK

What has four wheels and roars down the road?

A lion on a skateboard.

How do you fix a gorilla robot?

Use a monkey wrench.

What has four wheels and flies?

A garbage truck.

Why don't bananas get lonely?

They go around in bunches.

What is it called when a queen has a sore throat?

A royal pain in the neck.

How does a baker get rich?

He makes a lot of dough.

What do you do when an 800-pound gorilla asks you to dance?

Run.

Why did the mother bunny take her baby to the doctor?

He was feeling a little jumpy.

How do you stop a fish from smelling?

Put a clothespin on its nose.

Where does an otter put its money?

In a riverbank.

What is harder to catch the faster you run?

Your breath.

What room has no window, no door, and no walls?

A mushroom.

Why did the orange lose the race?

It ran out of juice.

Why does the ocean roar?

It has crabs in its bed.

What did the egg say to the cook?

You crack me up!